Copyright © 2024
Written by Kristan Hypolite M. Ed.

ISBN-13: 979-8-9912063-1-0

All rights reserved. No part of this book may be reproduced in any form without permission from the author or publisher, except as permitted by U.S. copyright law.

Illustrations Copyright © Kristan Hypolite M. Ed.

Book Design and Illustrations by by Uzuri Designs
www.uzuridesignsbooks.com
bookdesigner@uzuridesignsbooks.com

AFRICAN QUEENS

WRITTEN BY KRISTAN HYPOLITE M. ED.

In honor of the first Queen of my life, Mom, and Queens Deneka and Ayana, and future Queens Amaya, Naima, and Demi.

Thank you for all your love and support Queen Sasha, Queen Kazmin, Queen Octavia, Queen Rahel, family and friends.

PREFACE

As Kaleb turned three, life was filled with mystery. It all started when Kaleb explored grandma's living room and discovered a collage of family photos. Kaleb would always ask questions about family, where they lived, what their lives were like and what happened to them. I would often ask those same questions about our history.

His thirst for knowledge only grew stronger which ignited my passion about our history. Together delving into albums, books and documentaries, we continued to uncover mysteries of life past and present with our curiosity as our guiding light.

I admire historical figures like Mansa Musa, Frederick Douglas, Carter G. Woodson, and Marcus Garvey for their contributions to society and commitment to advancing social change. Their stories inspire me to strive for greatness in everything that I do.

I believe exploring cultures and customs around the world expands our knowledge of our past to help us navigate our present and shape our future.

TABLE OF CONTENTS

PREFACE VI
QUEEN AMANIRENAS 1
QUEEN AMINA 2
QUEEN BAKWA 3
QUEEN CLEOPATRA VII 4
QUEEN GUDIT 6
QUEEN HANGBE 7
QUEEN HATSHEPSUT 8
QUEEN IDIA 9
QUEEN ISIS 10
QUEEN KANDAKE 12
QUEEN MKABAYI KAJAMA 13
QUEEN MANTATISI 15
QUEEN MANGOU 16
QUEEN MAKEDA (QUEEN OF SHEBA) 18
QUEEN MUHUMUZA 19
QUEEN NEFERTITI 20
QUEEN NZINGA 21
QUEEN NANDI 22
QUEEN NEHANDA 23
QUEEN POKOU 24
QUEEN RIRIKUMUTIMA 25

QUEEN SEH-DONG-HONG-BEH	26
QUEEN TAYTU	27
QUEEN UWILINGIYIMANA	28
QUEEN WOIZERO	29
QUEEN YAA	30
QUEEN YOKO	31
QUEEN ZEWDITU	32
ABOUT THE AUTHOR	35
ABOUT THE BOOK	36
REFERENCES	37

QUEEN AMANIRENAS

Queen Amanirenas was one of the bravest one-eyed Kandake (Candace) of the Kingdom of Kush, now modern-day Sudan. In 30 BC, Amanirenas defeated an invasion by Patronius, the Roman governor of Egypt and sacked the city of Cyrene. Amanirenas was one of the most famous Kandakes, especially for leading Kushite armies in a war against the Romans from 27 BC to 22 BC.

QUEEN AMINA

Queen Amina was one of the greatest warriors of the Zaria Emirates, now modern-day Nigeria. Those cities are known as "Ganuwar of Amina" or "Amina's Walls." Amina was crowned Queen of Zazzau in 1576 AD. During her reign, which lasted 34 years, she expanded her kingdom's boundaries down to the Atlantic coast, founded several cities, and personally led an army of 20,000 soldiers to numerous battles. Today, she is remembered as "Amina Yar Bakwa, ta sa rana." meaning "Amina, daughter of Nikatau, a woman as capable as a man."

QUEEN BAKWA

Queen Bakwa was the first and one of the greatest warriors of the Zaria Emirates, now modern-day Nigeria. In 1536 AD, she founded the city of Zaria in North Central Nigeria, and named it after her younger daughter. Her two daughters, Amina and Zaria, would rule after her death.

QUEEN CLEOPATRA VII

Queen Cleopatra VII was one of the greatest political figures of Ancient Egypt, now modern-day Egypt. After her father King Ptolemy XII died, she and her brother ascended to the throne. When Cleopatra was 18 years old, she assembled an army to overthrow her brother. She defeated him in the Battle of the Nile, with help from Julius Caesar of Rome. Historians believe that when Julius sought refuge in Egypt during Rome's civil war, they had a child together named Caesarion.

QUEEN GUDIT

Queen Gudit was one of the greatest Kandake (Candace) of the Kingdom of Axum, now modern-day Ethiopia. Gudit (Ge'ez: ጉዲት), also known as Yodit, was a legendary Queen from Semien. (fl. c. 960AD). According to local legend, Gudit laid waste to the Kingdom of Aksum by destroying churches, monuments, and attempting to exterminate the ruling dynasty.

In 937 AD, Gudit (Judith), Queen of Falash, attacked Axum, the sacred capital of Ethiopia, killing all the inhabitants, including the descendants of King Solomon and the Queen of Sheba. There is a tradition that Gudit sacked and burned Debre Damo, an amba, which at the time was a treasury and a prison for the male relatives of the king. This tradition may be an echo of the later capture and sack of Amba Geshen by Ahmad ibn Ibrahim al-Ghazi. Gudit is known as "Esato" from the word "Esat" in Amharic, which means "fire".

QUEEN HANGBE

Queen Hangbe was Ruler and Queen of the Dahomey Kingdom, now modern-day Benin. She was an Amazonian born into royalty with her twin brother, Akaba. When her brother died in battle, Hangbe held down the war front. Her legacy lives on in the story of the Dahomey Amazon women.

DAHOMEY KINGDOM

QUEEN HATSHEPSUT

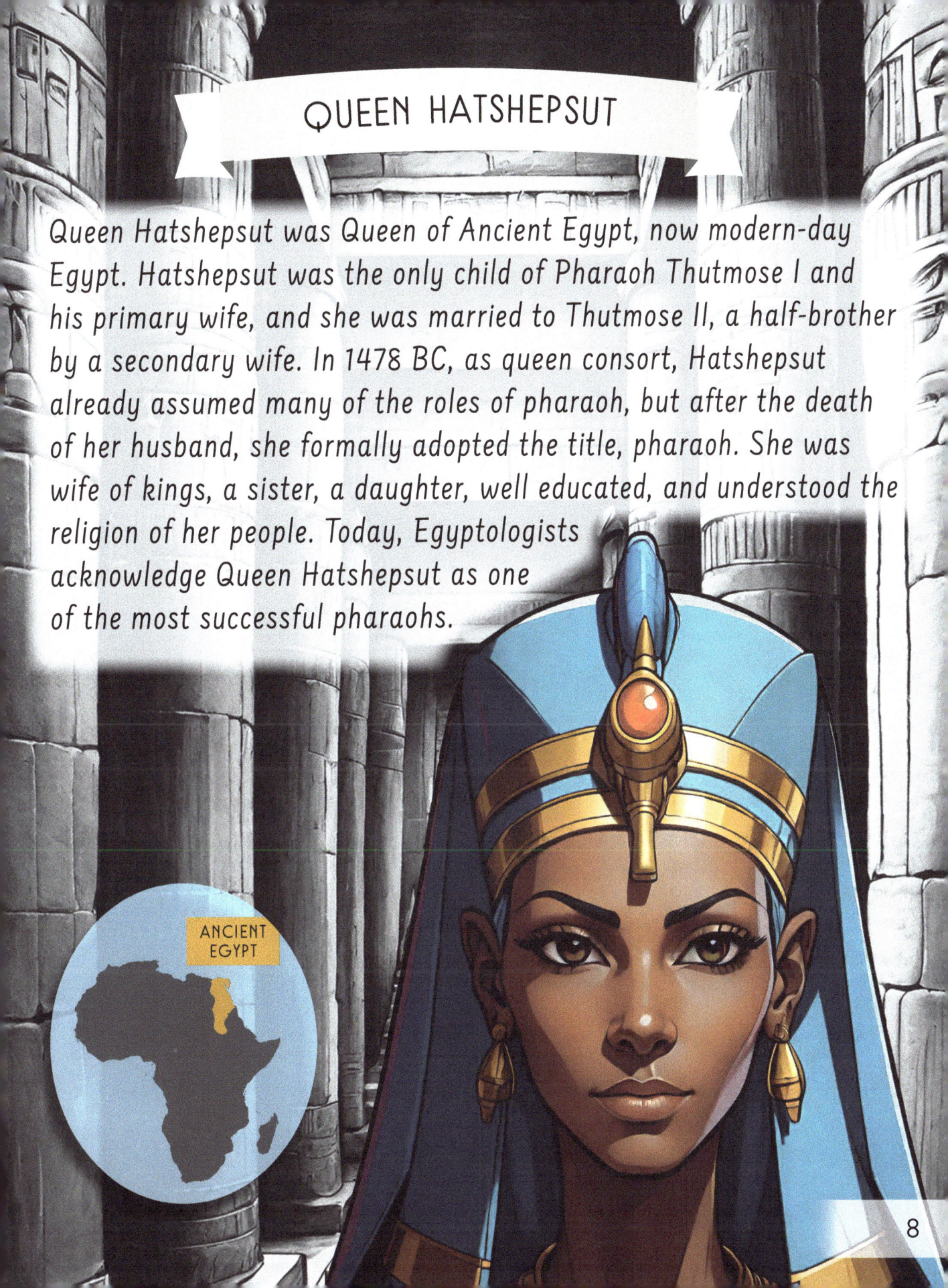

Queen Hatshepsut was Queen of Ancient Egypt, now modern-day Egypt. Hatshepsut was the only child of Pharaoh Thutmose I and his primary wife, and she was married to Thutmose II, a half-brother by a secondary wife. In 1478 BC, as queen consort, Hatshepsut already assumed many of the roles of pharaoh, but after the death of her husband, she formally adopted the title, pharaoh. She was wife of kings, a sister, a daughter, well educated, and understood the religion of her people. Today, Egyptologists acknowledge Queen Hatshepsut as one of the most successful pharaohs.

QUEEN IDIA

Queen Idia was an Army General of the Benin Kingdom, now modern-day Nigeria. Queen Idia was the first woman who went to and fought in war. She used her magical powers and knowledge of medicine to help her son overcome his enemies. She was one of the best known female soldiers ever from the Benin Kingdom. She was a fearless Army General who led the Armies of Benin on several successful battles.

QUEEN ISIS

Queen Isis was Queen of Ancient Egypt, now modern-day Egypt. Isis was the most famous and powerful goddess in the Egyptian pantheon. Today, the statue above Cairo Museum depicting Isis suckling the baby Horus, is considered by many to be the original "Madonna and Child."

QUEEN KANDAKE

Queen Kandake (Candace) was a fierce, tactical and uniting military leader in Ethiopia. Kandake was regarded as one of the most dreaded war generals of her time.

During that era, the meaning of Candace was "Queen Mother" or "Royal Woman." Candaces were warriors and did not reign with men. There were as many as eight Candaces of Meroe.

Shanakdakhete (r.c. 150 BCE - 170 BCE)
Amanirenas (r.c. 40 BCE - 10 BCE)
Amanishakheto (r.c. 10 BCE -1 CE)
Amanitore (r.c. 1 CE - 25 CE)
Amantitere (r.c. 25 CE - 41 CE)
Amanikhatashan (r.c. 62 CE - 85 CE)
Maleqorobar (r.c. 266 CE - 283 CE)
Lahideamani (r.c. 306 CE - 314 CE)

A "Candace, queen of the Ethiopians" is mentioned in the Bible when the apostle Philip meets "a eunuch of great authority" under her reign and converts him to Christianity (Acts 8:27-39). In this passage, as in other ancient works mentioning Candace, the royal title, has often been confused with a personal name.

QUEEN MKABAYI KAJAMA

Queen Mkabayi KaJama was Queen of the Zulu Kingdom, now modern-day South Africa. Mkabayi KaJama (c. 1750 AD - 1843 AD) was founder and the head of the Qulusi military kraal and Regent of the Zulu. She persuaded her father, the Zulu King Jama kaNdaba, to remarry, and acted as a regent to her ensuing half-brother, Senzangakhona. She was a kingmaker for three succeeding reigns, leading coups and arranging assassinations. She is credited for bringing stability in the Zulu nation and ensuring the continuation of the Zulu line and monarchy.

QUEEN MANTATISI

Queen Mantatisi was Queen of the baTlokwas, now modern-day South Africa. In the 1800s, Mantatisi, warrior Queen of the baTlokwas fought to preserve her tribal lands during wars between Shaka Zulu and Matiwane. She succeeded in protecting the baTlokwas heritage although her son, who became King when she died, was eventually defeated by Mahweshwe.

QUEEN MANGOU

Queen Mangou was Queen of the Mauori people or Azna community, now modern-day Niger. Sarrounia, meaning "Queen or female chief" in Hausa language, mobilized the Azna community against French powers unlike the men around her. The French eventually retreated from battle with Sarrounia Mangou leading her troops. Despite what has been written or not, her lineage lives on.

QUEEN MAKEDA
(QUEEN OF SHEBA)

Queen Makeda "Queen of Sheba" was Queen of the Kingdom of Axum, later called Kingdom of Sheba, now modern-day Ethiopia. Ethiopia's 14th-century royal epic, the Kebra Nagast or "Glory of Kings," writes that Makeda was a queen of incredible strength.

According to the epic, she survived a battle with the serpent King Awre. The serpent king was troubling the northern Ethiopian Kingdom of Axum. After defeating the serpent king, Makeda became the Queen of Axum.

Makeda is famous for her story with the biblical figure, King Solomon of Jerusalem. They had a son named Menelik I (Ebna la-Hakim), meaning "son of the wise." Their son became the first imperial ruler of Ethiopia and the first of a line of Aksûmite kings. According to historians, Makeda and her son brought back the biblical Ark of the Covenant to Axum. Through them, the lineage of great East African and Nubian kings were born.

She left a legacy as an essential figure in Old Testament history for the Ethiopian Orthodox Church.

QUEEN MUHUMUZA

Queen Muhumuza was an influential leader of the East African Nyabingi spiritual practice in Rwanda and Uganda from 1850 AD to 1950 AD. Muhumuza is said to have been a medium of the spirit of a legendary African woman, known as Nyabinghi. According to some Rwandan sources, her original name was Muserakande. She was married to Kigeri Rwabugiri, King of Rwanda from 1867 AD to 1895 AD and they had a son named Biregeya.

QUEEN NEFERTITI

Queen Nefertiti was Queen of the Kingdom of Kush, now modern-day Egypt. Queen Nefertiti was a prominent queen from Ancient Egypt. Her name means "a beautiful woman has come." She left a legacy of strength, power, and beauty.

QUEEN NZINGA

Queen Nzinga (Mbande Zinga) was Queen of Ndongo, now modern-day Angola. Mbande Zinga was the sister and advisor of the King of Ngola and served as his representative in negotiating treaties with the Portuguese. In 1624 AD, her brother died and she became Queen Nzinga. She appointed women, including her sister Kifunji and Mukumbu, to all government offices.

When the Portuguese broke the peace treaty, Mbande led her largely female army against them inflicting terrible casualties. She conquered nearby kingdoms to build a mighty confederation to drive the Portuguese out of Africa. In 1635 AD, Nzinga accepted a truce and then agreed to a peace treaty. After settling disputes and waging long wars, Nzinga allied her nation with the Dutch, marking the first African-European alliance against a European oppressor. In 1975, Angola became an independent nation and a street was named in her honor.

QUEEN NANDI

Queen Nandi was Queen of Zululand, later Zulu Kingdom, now modern-day South Africa. Queen Nandi was the mother of Shaka Zulu, one of Zulu Kingdom's greatest kings. The Zulu nation was a superpower in the South African region. Queen Nandi's story is one of resilience as a mother, and one of hope against social pressures.

QUEEN NEHANDA

Queen Nehanda was Queen of the MaShona Kingdom, now modern-day Zimbabwe. Nehanda was one of Zimbabwe's youngest and most influential religious leaders. She declared war when the English invaded their country. Nehanda remains the single most important person in the history of Zimbabwe.

MaSHONA KINGDOM

QUEEN POKOU

Queen Pokou was Queen of the Baoule tribe, a subgroup of the Akan people, later called Ashanti Empire, now modern-day Ghana. After sacrificing her son to reign as Princess Abla Pokou, she led a breakaway group of the Ashanti Empire on a long journey to build their own tribe. After creating the Baoule tribe, she passed away leaving her niece to take the throne.

QUEEN RIRIKUMUTIMA

Queen Ririkumutima was Queen of the Burundi Kingdom, modern-day Burundi. She was the daughter of Chief Sekawonyi and Inankinso and the 13th wife of King Mwezi Gisabo. Ririkumutima was known for her quest to be Queen Mother, who killed Ntibahinya, her co-wife and the mother of the crown prince. She claimed that she was the biological mother of crown Prince Mbukije and thus the rightful regent during Prince Mbukije and Mwambutsa IV reign. As Queen Mother and regent, Ririkumutima was very influential and was described as "intelligent, as energetic and more stubborn than all the princes in her entourage."

BURUNDI

QUEEN SEH-DONG-HONG-BEH

Queen Seh-Dong-Hong-Beh was Queen of the Dahomey Kingdom, modern-day Benin. Seh-Dong-Hong-Beh was a leader of the Dahomey under King Gezo. In 1851 AD, she led an army of 6,000 women against the Egba fortress of Abeokuta.

QUEEN TAYTU

Queen Taytu was Queen of Ethiopia. Taytu was the Empress of Ethiopia and established the capital of modern-day Ethiopia, Addis Ababa. As a loyal queen and brilliant military strategist, Empress Taytu was equal to her reigning husband, Emperor Menelik II. For over 14 years, Taytu led troops in battle while negotiating peace treaties. She forged battle plans that led to many victories for Ethiopia as they rose to freedom.

QUEEN UWILINGIYIMANA

Queen Uwilingiyimana was Queen of the MaShona Kingdom, modern-day Rwanda. Uwilingiyimana, known as Madame Agathe, served as a Prime Minister of Rwanda and acting president from 18 July 1993 AD until her assassination on 7 April 1994 AD, during the opening stages of the Rwandan genocide. She was Rwanda's first and so far only female prime minister.

QUEEN WOIZERO

Queen Woizero was Queen of the Ethiopian Empire, now modern-day Ethiopia. She was the Empress consort and wife of Tafari Makonnen, known as Haile Selassie I, Emperor of Ethiopia. The account given in the "Autobiography of the Emperor, My Life and Ethiopia's Progress", stated that at the age of 20, they were married by their own mutual consent and described her as "a woman without any malice whatsoever."

QUEEN YAA

Queen Yaa Asantewaa was Queen of the Ashanti Empire, now modern-day Ghana. Queen Yaa heroically fought against British colonizers until she was exiled. History indicates that she used her oratory skills to inspire village chiefs to fight back against colonialists and encouraged her people to take up arms to fight for the release of King Prempeh. Ghana celebrates Queen Asantewaa as the last African woman to lead a decisive battle against colonialists as a national holiday.

QUEEN YOKO

Queen Yoko was Queen of the Kpe Mende Confederacy, now modern-day Sierra Leone. Madame Yoko ruled and led an army of fourteen tribes. At that time, 15% of all tribes were led by women. Kpe Mende Confederacy was the largest tribal group of the 19th century. Today, approximately 9% of tribes have women rulers.

QUEEN ZEWDITU

Queen Zewditu was Queen of the Ethiopian Empire, now modern-day Ethiopia. Zewditu (ዘውዲቱ;Zäwditu) born as Askala Maryam was the first female head of an internationally recognized country in Africa as Empress Regnant of the Ethiopian Empire from 1916 AD to 1930 AD. Her reign was noted for reforms of her Regent and designated heir Ras Tafari Makonnen, who succeeded her as Emperor Haile Selassie I.

Due to her staunch conservatism and strong religious devotion, she was at best ambivalent and often stridently opposed. As of 2020 AD, Zewditu is the most recent empress regnant in history.

HER LEGACY CONTINUES...

All of these Queens have stories of fighting wars, changing nations, and lived boldly despite their environments so many decades and centuries ago.

from Queen Mangou

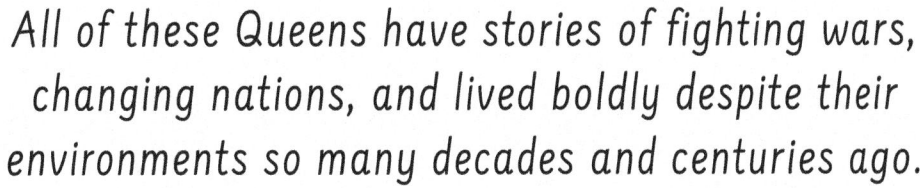

ABOUT THE AUTHOR

My name is Kristan Hypolite, M. Ed. I am the proud father of Kaleb Hypolite, an enthusiastic educator, and an entrepreneur.

As a father, I am amazed by Kaleb's brilliant and witty personality. We keep our mind sharp by playing chess, checkers, and puzzles. We stay active by playing basketball, flag football, and soccer.

In addition to sports and recreation, we have a keen interest in traveling, world history and music, especially Afro beats, reggae, and soca. We find these activities not only bring us joy but help us relax and unwind.

As an educator with a Masters Degree in Special Education, I am committed to providing a nurturing and inclusive learning environment for all future kings and queens. I believe they are capable of achieving greatness with the proper resources and supports.

As an entrepreneur, I'm dedicated to teaching principles and providing access to resources for all kings and queens to establish generational wealth.

ABOUT THE BOOK

African Queens have shaped our civilization and history for centuries. As mothers of humanity, warrior queens, and queen mothers of empires, African women have been extraordinary leaders from the beginning of civilization to present-day.

From Queen Amanirenas, leading Kushite armies against the Romans to Queen Uwilingiyimana, Rwanda's first female prime minister, these awesome women are examples of leadership. African Queens untold story is a story that connects cultures near and far and embody humanity around the world.

REFERENCES

1. 10 Of Africa's Most Formidable Warrior Queens-African Vibes Magazine - https://www.africanvibes.com/10-brave-african-warrior-queens/
2. Amanirenas - Wikipedia - https://en.wikipedia.org/wiki/Amanirenas
3. Queen Bakwa of Turunku - African Heritage (afrolegends.com) - https://afrolegends.com/tag/queen-bakwa-of-turunku/
4. Legend of the Crown: The Art of African Kings and Queens- Kentake Page - https://kentakepage.com/legend-of-the-crown-the-art-of-african-kings-and-queens/
5. Queens & Women Warriors of Africa (geni.com) - https://www.geni.com/projects/Queens-Women-Warriors-of-Africa/14190
6. 11 Real African Queens to Name Your Daughter After – AfriQueen Media - http://afriqueenmedia.com/news/names-daughter
7. Legend of the Crown: The Art of African Kings and Queens - Kentake Page - https://kentakepage.com/legend-of-the-crown-the-art-of-african-kings-and-queens/
8. Famous African queens and goddesses - museumafricaproject (google.com) - https://sites.google.com/site/museumafricaproject/famous-african-queens-and-goddesses
9. Early African Women: Hunters, Warriors, & Rulers - America's Black Holocaust Museum (abhmuseum.org) - https://www.abhmuseum.org/early-african-women-hunters-warriors-rulers
10. Mkabayi kaJama - Wikipedia - https://en.wikipedia.org/wiki/Mkabayi_kaJama
11. 10 Of Africa's Most Formidable Warrior Queens - African Vibes Magazine - https://www.africanvibes.com/10-brave-african-warrior-queens/

12. Famous African queens and goddesses - museumafricaproject (google.com) - https://sites.google.com/site/museumafricaproject/famous-african-queens-and-goddesses
13. Early African Women: Hunters, Warriors, & Rulers - America's Black Holocaust Museum (abhmuseum.org) - https://www.abhmuseum.org/early-african-women-hunters-warriors-rulers/
14. Five African queens you did not know existed - Page 5 of 6 - Face2Face Africa - https://face2faceafrica.com/article/five-african-queens-you-did-not-know-existed/5
15. Agathe Uwilingiyimana - Wikipedia - https://en.wikipedia.org/wiki/Agathe_Uwilingiyimana
16. Menen Asfaw - Wikipedia - https://en.wikipedia.org/wiki/Menen_Asfaw
17. 5 Most Influential African Queens in History (face2faceafrica.com) - https://face2faceafrica.com/article/5-most-influential-african-queens-in-history/6
18. Zewditu - Wikipedia - https://en.wikipedia.org/wiki/Zewditu

www.ingramcontent.com/pod-product-compliance
Lightning Source LLC
Chambersburg PA
CBHW051327110526
44582CB00003B/78